This book belongs to:

Lacey

It was given to me by:

Katie McDonald

On:

Oct. 2, 2005

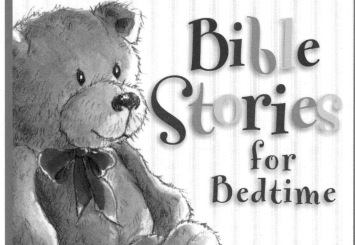

Bible Stories
for Bedtime

Terry Brown

ILLUSTRATED BY DOUG SMITH

BARBOUR
PUBLISHING

Published by Barbour Publishing, Inc., P.O. Box 719, Uhrichsville, Ohio 44683, www.barbourbooks.com

Our mission is to publish and distribute inspirational products offering exceptional value and biblical encouragement to the masses.

 Member of the
Evangelical Christian
Publishers Association

Printed in China.
5 4 3 2 1

To all my little friends
who are growing in God's Word.

Contents

As parents, many of our most cherished memories are of our children's firsts—their first smile, their first words, their first steps. The first of anything they do seems so remarkable and worthy of remembering. This book, *Bible Stories for Bedtime,* will help you capture, for years to come, the wonder of a little one who is first experiencing the Word of God.

Created for children ages two to five, *Bible Stories for Bedtime* shares colorful and engaging Bible stories that introduce God's eternal heroes—and plant the seeds of a lasting faith. Also included are "My Prayers" and "God's Promises," both written in words children will understand, as well as the thoughtful "Snuggle Sessions." These specially designed questions connect kids with the stories and encourage conversations within families—and the writing space that follows allows you as a parent to record your children's first thoughts about God.

It is my hope that this book will nestle into the hearts of children, offering God's truth and light for their lives, while also serving as a treasured keepsake for parents.

Terry Brown

Genesis 1

God Creates the World

LORD, THANK YOU FOR THE BEAUTIFUL
WORLD YOU CREATED. . . .

In the beginning darkness, there was nothing! But,
when I said, "Let there be light," there was light!
I created this beautiful world.

Everything you see I designed for you. I made the earth and the oceans, the blue sky and the warm sun. I made the bright moon and the twinkling stars, the valleys and the mountains. Then in a land called the Garden of Eden, I placed beautiful plants, colorful flowers, and all the fruits.

Next came all the animals: the bears and the lions, the elephants and the giraffes, the kittens and the puppies, the birds and all the crawly bugs. But something was missing. I needed a helper and a friend to care for all of My creations.

So I took the dust on the ground and made a person I named Adam. And just like that, Adam became alive!

Snuggle Session

God made many special things for us to enjoy. He made flowers, trees, and animals. What is your favorite thing God made?

_____

_____

_____

_____

What are some special things about you?

_____

_____

_____

Bible Stories for Bedtime

My Prayer

Thank You, God, for making so many beautiful things.
Thank You for the flowers, stars, and animals. But
most of all, thank You for making me.

God's Promise

"Look up toward the sky. Who created
everything you see?" — ISAIAH 40:26

Genesis 6–9

The Great Flood

DEAR GOD, HELP ME STAY PURE
AND BLAMELESS LIKE NOAH. . . .

The earth grew quickly but with very bad people.
My heart ached with sadness. I felt sorry that I had
ever created people. So I planned to start over and
get rid of all bad living things, both human beings

and animals. I chose a special man to help. His name was Noah. Noah loved Me and listened to My voice.

I told Noah to prepare for a great flood by building a big boat called an ark! Soon water would rain from the sky and flood the land. The water would drown everything. . .everything except Noah, his family, and two of every animal. Noah trusted Me. He did what I told him. He built an ark that would carry his family and all the animals high above the water.

One day the rain poured from the sky. It rained for forty days and forty nights. What I had said would happen did. And after the waters disappeared, I placed a beautiful rainbow in the sky and made a promise to Noah. "I will never again destroy the earth with a flood."

So when you see a rainbow in the sky, remember the promise I made to Noah.

Snuggle Session

How do you feel when you see rain?

_____

_____

_____

_____

What do you think it would have been like to be with Noah on the ark?

_____

_____

_____

_____

How do you feel when you see God's promise, the rainbow?

_____

_____

_____

My Prayer

Dear God, thank You for this world You made. Help me to live a life that makes You happy.

God's Promise

"I have put my rainbow in the clouds. It will be the sign of the covenant between me and the earth." — GENESIS 9:13

Genesis 15–18, 21

God's New Promise to Abraham

LORD, THANK YOU FOR THE MANY
GIFTS YOU GIVE ME. . . .

After the flood, the earth sprouted with new people
and I continued with My plan. I told another friend,
Abraham, to move to a new land.

20

"Take your wife, Sarah, and everything you own and move to the land of Canaan. I am going to make your family so big it will stretch all over the world."

Abraham listened and set off on his new journey. One night, when the stars filled the sky, I promised Abraham a great gift.

I said, "Abraham, look at all the stars. That is how many people will be in the family I am going to give you."

Abraham believed me, but he wondered how this could be. "Lord, I have no son, and I'm growing to be an old man!"

When Abraham's wife, Sarah, heard the news, she laughed. But Abraham believed; and after many years of waiting, his son was born. He named him Isaac.

Snuggle Session

How do you think you would feel if you had to leave all your friends like Abraham did?

_____

_____

_____

_____

God promised Abraham a son. God makes promises to us, too. Some of God's promises are. . .

_____

_____

_____

_____

My Prayer

Lord, thank You for the many gifts You give me.

God's Promise

"The Lord is faithful and will keep all of his promises." — PSALM 145:13

The Sons of Isaac

THANK YOU, GOD, FOR GIVING
ME YOUR BLESSINGS. . . .

When Isaac grew up, he married
Rebekah. I blessed them with twin boys!
The first baby son, Esau, was very hairy. And the second son, Jacob, had smooth skin.

As the boys grew, Isaac loved Esau and Rebekah loved Jacob. One day Isaac called for Esau. "Esau, I am getting old, and I do not know the day that I will die. Go and bring me something good to eat. Then I will give you my blessing before I die." Obeying his father, Esau took his bow and arrow and left.

Rebekah overheard the conversation and went to Jacob. "Jacob, listen to me, and do what I command. I will prepare some food, and you will take it to your father so you may receive the blessing."

"But, Mother, I am not hairy like Esau. Father will know that I have tricked him and curse me," replied Jacob.

Rebekah took animal fur and some of Esau's clothes and put them on Jacob. Then she gave the food to her son, and he went to his father.

"Are you really Esau?" asked Isaac. "Then bring my food so you may receive my blessing." Jacob bent down and Isaac kissed him. Isaac smelled his clothes and touched the hairy fur. Isaac believed he was speaking to Esau and gave Jacob his blessing.

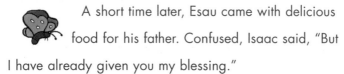 A short time later, Esau came with delicious food for his father. Confused, Isaac said, "But I have already given you my blessing."

"No, you haven't, Father," said Esau. "That was my brother. He tricked you!"

Isaac couldn't give Esau the same blessing he gave Jacob, so Esau received a different one. But in his blessing, Isaac said that Esau would always serve his younger brother, Jacob. From then on, Esau hated Jacob.

Snuggle Session

Jacob tricked Isaac and stole his brother's blessing. How would you feel if someone stole something important from you?

_____

_____

_____

Esau hated Jacob because of his actions. How can you make sure your actions do not get you in trouble?

_____

_____

_____

My Prayer

Dear God, help me to trust You to give me everything I need.

God's Promise

"Those who act wisely prove that wisdom is right." — MATTHEW 11:19

Genesis 29

Jacob Finds a Wife

DEAR LORD, HELP ME NOT TO RUN
FROM MY TROUBLES. . . .

When he realized Esau wanted to kill him, Jacob
ran away from home. He went far away to his Uncle
Laban's home. Jacob met his cousin Rachel and soon
fell in love. He wanted to marry her.

"Jacob, you can marry my daughter if you work for me seven years," said Uncle Laban. Jacob agreed. He worked for Laban seven long years. Then he was ready to marry Rachel.

But Rachel had an older sister named Leah. Leah also needed a husband. So Laban fooled Jacob into marrying Leah first.

Jacob was angry! "What have you done to me?" he screamed.

"Don't worry," said Laban. "I will still let you marry Rachel. . .for another seven years of hard work."

Jacob loved Rachel so much that he agreed. So Jacob worked seven more years to marry her.

Snuggle Session

How do you feel when you don't get something you want?

_____

_____

_____

_____

Things that make me angry:

_____

_____

_____

_____

My Prayer

Dear God, help me to not run away from my troubles.

God's Promise

"The Lord is a place of safety for those who have been beaten down. He keeps them safe in times of trouble." — PSALM 9:9

Genesis 37, 42–45

Joseph Is Sold to Strangers

THANK YOU, LORD, FOR NEVER
LEAVING MY SIDE. . . .

Abraham's family continued to be My special people.
But Joseph, one of Jacob and Rachel's sons, had a
tough life. His father gave him a beautiful colored coat,
and his brothers hated him because of it. They were

jealous of the special attention he got from their father.

One day while working in the fields, the brothers decided to get rid of Joseph. "Look, here comes Joseph," they said. "Let's throw him into a big hole and tell Father a wild animal killed him."

"We shouldn't kill him," said the oldest brother, Reuben. "Let's think of something else."

Just then a group of strangers were traveling by. "Hey, look, let's sell Joseph to those strangers." The brothers all agreed. They grabbed Joseph, tore off his colored coat, and sold him to the strangers.

The brothers dipped the coat in animal's blood and told their father that a wild beast killed Joseph. Heartbroken, Jacob cried for days. But I took care of Joseph.

Years later there was no food except in Egypt. Jacob told his sons to travel to the distant land to buy food.

What a surprise they found! The man who decided who should get food turned out to be Joseph! Joseph forgave his brothers, and his whole family moved to Egypt to live near him.

Snuggle Session

Have you ever wanted a toy that belonged to someone else?

_____

_____

_____

_____

Joseph was very sad when his brothers sold him to the strangers. What makes you sad?

_____

_____

_____

_____

When Joseph's brothers came to him, he forgave them.
When have you shown love to someone who hurt you?

_____

_____

_____

My Prayer

Thank You, God, for never leaving my side.

God's Promise

"The Lord your God will go with you.
He will never leave you. He'll never
desert you." — DEUTERONOMY 31:6

Exodus 1–2

A Mother Hides Her Baby Son

I KNOW I AM ALWAYS SAFE IN YOUR
HANDS, GOD. . . .

Years later My special people, called Hebrews, still
lived in Egypt. But life was no longer as good for
them as it had been in Joseph's day. The evil king of

Egypt, Pharaoh, made a law that the Egyptians should kill all the baby Hebrew boys.

One Hebrew woman hid her baby son for three months. But soon the time came when she could not hide him any longer. "You are getting too big to hide. I must do something," said the boy's mother.

So she made a basket, placed her baby son inside it, and floated him down the Nile River. The boy's mother trusted Me to take care of him. And I did.

As the boy floated down the river in the basket, Pharaoh's daughter discovered him. "What is that floating in the river? Bring me the basket," she said to her maidservant.

Pharaoh's daughter opened the basket. "It's a baby!"

Immediately, she decided to raise the child as her own son. "I will give him the name Moses."

Moses grew to be a young prince. One day he saw an Egyptian hit a Hebrew slave. It made him so angry he killed the Egyptian. In fear of Pharaoh, Moses ran far away to the land of Midian.

Snuggle Session

Moses' mother hid him to keep him alive. What have you hidden? Why?

_____

_____

_____

_____

If you've ever seen a river, it can be big and scary. How would you feel if you had to cross a river by yourself?

_____

_____

_____

Bible Stories for Bedtime

My Prayer

Dear God, thank You for always being with me even in scary times.

God's Promise

"Your hand would always be there to guide me. Your right hand would still be holding me close." — PSALM 139:10

Exodus 3–4, 8–14

Moses Is Chosen

O GOD, THANK YOU FOR CHOOSING ME. . . .

Pharaoh, the king of Egypt, made the Hebrews slaves. The Hebrews, also called Israelites, prayed to Me to get them out of slavery.

One day while Moses was up in the mountains, I appeared to him in a flame of fire from a bush.

"What is this? The bush is on fire, but it isn't

burning up!" cried Moses.

"Moses, Moses, take off your sandals, for you are standing on holy ground," I said. "I am going to send you to bring My people out of Egypt."

"But, God, I do not know how to speak to Pharaoh! He would never listen to me. Please send somebody else," begged Moses.

But I chose Moses to do the job. So Moses traveled back to Egypt to free the slaves. Pharaoh gave Moses a hard time, but I gave Moses many signs to convince the king to let the Israelites go. Finally, Pharaoh did.

But after he let the Israelites go, Pharaoh changed his mind. He wanted his slaves back. So he and his army chased after them. I parted the water in the Red Sea for Moses and his people so they could get away from Pharaoh's army. But when Pharaoh and his men followed, I closed the sea around them and they drowned. Finally, Moses and the others rested at a mountain called Sinai. It was on this mountain I gave Moses the Ten Commandments.

Snuggle Session

Moses was afraid to go back to Egypt, but he knew he had to do what God told him to do. When have you felt afraid?

_____

_____

_____

God chose Moses to free His people. God has chosen you, too. How does it make you feel to know God has a special purpose for you?

_____

_____

_____

My Prayer

Thank You, God, for choosing me. Help me fulfill my purpose for You!

God's Promise

"You did not choose me. Instead, I chose you." — JOHN 15:16

Moses Is Chosen

43

Exodus 20

The Ten Commandments

I WILL ALWAYS TRY TO OBEY YOU, LORD. . . .

1. I am the Lord your God. You shall have no other gods before Me.

2. You shall not have any idols or worship them.

3. You shall never misuse the name of God.

4. Keep the Sabbath day holy. You shall rest on this holy day.

5. Honor and obey your father and mother.

6. You shall not kill anyone.

7. You shall not break a marriage vow.

8. You shall not steal.

9. You shall not say false statements about your neighbors.

10. You shall not desire your neighbors' possessions.

Snuggle Session

God gave us the Ten Commandments to help us know how to live. What are things your mommy and daddy might say to keep you safe?

_____

_____

_____

How do you feel about rules that your parents make you obey?

_____

_____

_____

My Prayer

Thank You, God, for loving me so much that You gave me rules to keep me safe.

God's Promise

"If you want to enter the kingdom, obey the commandments." — MATTHEW 19:17

Exodus 16

The Lord Gives Manna

LORD, HELP ME TO TRUST YOU. . . .

When Moses led the Israelites in the desert, I traveled with them. During the day My presence looked like a cloud. At night My presence looked like a pillar of fire.

After being in the desert for many days, the Israelites began to complain. They said they didn't have enough to eat. They were angry with Moses for leading them out of slavery because they were hungry.

Finally, I told Moses that I had heard their complaints. I decided to give them something to eat. So every morning I left flakes of food, called manna, on the ground. The Israelites collected enough for everyone in each family. On Saturday every family was to collect two days' worth of manna so that they would not have to work on Sunday.

And for forty years, the Israelites ate manna from heaven until they arrived in the promised land.

Snuggle Session

God gave food to the Israelites when they were waiting to find the promised land. How does God provide you with food?

_____

_____

_____

_____

What is your favorite food to eat?

_____

_____

_____

My Prayer

Thank You, God, for giving me food so that I may grow bigger to serve You better.

God's Promise

"Give thanks to the Lord. Worship him. Tell the nations what he has done."

— 1 CHRONICLES 16:8

Deuteronomy 34–Joshua 1–6

Joshua Takes the Lead

LORD, I WANT TO BE A LEADER LIKE JOSHUA.
GUIDE ME. . . .

Because the Israelites were stubborn, they did not

listen to Me. They wandered in the wilderness for

forty years. I took Moses to the top of a mountain and

showed him the land called Canaan beyond the Jordan River. I promised Moses the Israelites would someday live in this land. Soon after this, Moses died. Then I chose Joshua to finish leading the Israelites to the new land. I told Joshua, "Do not be afraid, for I am with you wherever you go."

But trouble wasn't far away. I told Joshua, "Capture the city of Jericho." I told Joshua exactly what to do in order to capture the city. "You and your men shall march around the city for six days. Seven priests shall carry trumpets. And on the seventh day, you shall march around the city seven times. Then the priests shall blow their trumpets."

Joshua obeyed Me. The horns blew and the Israelites shouted. The walls of Jericho fell down, and the city was captured. Joshua and his army destroyed everything in the city.

Snuggle Session

The Israelites had to walk, lost, in the desert for forty years because they didn't listen to God. How can you listen to God?

_____

_____

_____

How do you think it would have been to hear all of the trumpets blow and see the walls of Jericho come crashing down?

_____

_____

_____

My Prayer

Thank You, God, for keeping Your promises.

God's Promise

"The Lord says, 'I will save the one who loves me. I will keep him safe because he trusts in me.'" — PSALM 91:14

Judges 6–7

Gideon Tests God

TEST MY HEART, O LORD. . . .

Many years went by for My people when once
again, they had to go to battle. This time they were in
the hands of their enemy, the Midianites. I picked
Gideon, the mighty warrior, to fight this battle.

But Gideon questioned Me. "Lord, how can I do

this? I am so weak. Give me a sign that it is really You talking to me. One more request, just to be sure!" Gideon kept asking Me to prove I was real, and I gave many signs. Finally, he believed.

Gideon had a tough task ahead of him. The Midianites were strong and mighty. Gideon had a large army, but I told him to send thousands home. I wanted to prove to the Israelites that they would win the battle because of Me, not because of their many soldiers. I left only three hundred soldiers to fight the battle against the Midianites. The Israelites' only weapons were trumpets and pitchers. They surrounded the Midianites in the night. They listened to Me, and at the right time the soldiers blew their horns, broke the pitchers, and fought against their enemy. All the noise filled the Midianites with fear. And because Gideon trusted Me, the Israelites won the battle!

Snuggle Session

I know God loves me because. . .

_____

_____

_____

_____

God helps us every day. How has God helped

you today?

_____

_____

_____

_____

My Prayer

Dear God, thank You for taking care of me when I obey You.

God's Promise

"Anyone who has my commands and obeys them loves me. My Father will love the one who loves me. I too will love him."

— JOHN 14:21

Judges 13–16

Samson's Strength Is Lost

THANK YOU FOR THE STRENGTH
YOU HAVE GIVEN ME. . . .

Samson was special. I loved him, and he loved Me.
When Samson was born, his mother promised Me she
would never cut his hair. This made him different from
others. His long hair became a sign to his people and

his enemies, the Philistines, that he was different. The longer his hair grew, the stronger Samson grew. I gave him his strength!

But sin filled Samson's heart. He loved a woman named Delilah, and the Philistines knew this.

"Delilah, help us capture Samson, and we will give you a lot of money," demanded the enemy. Delilah agreed.

"Samson, please tell me the secret of your strength," pleaded Delilah.

Although Samson knew he shouldn't tell Delilah, after several pleas he gave in to her request. "If my hair is cut, I will lose my strength."

That night Delilah cut Samson's hair and told his enemies. And the Philistines captured Samson.

In the end, I heard Samson's cries for revenge against the Philistines. I gave him strength one last time. And with Samson's last request, he pushed against the pillars of the temple and crushed all the people, including himself.

Snuggle Session

God gave Samson a special gift when He gave him his great strength. What's the best gift you have ever received?

_____

_____

_____

_____

Who gave you that gift?

_____

_____

_____

_____

How would that person have felt if you threw the gift away like Samson did with God's gift?

_____

_____

_____

My Prayer

Thank You, God, for the strength You give me through Your love. Help me to always do what pleases You.

God's Promise

"But God gives you the gift of eternal life because of what Christ Jesus our Lord has done." — ROMANS 6:23

Ruth

Ruth Marries Boaz

I BELONG TO YOU, LORD. . . .

When Ruth's husband died, she had a decision to make. She had to decide whether to find another husband or to travel back to Judah with her mother-in-law, Naomi. Ruth loved Naomi. She felt as though

they belonged together, no matter what. So she chose to go with Naomi.

"Wherever you go, I will go. Your people will be my people and your God my God," Ruth told her mother-in-law. Even though it might have been easier for Ruth to stay in Moab, she wanted to be with Naomi and My people.

After she moved to Judah, Ruth met a man named Boaz. Boaz was kind to Ruth because of all she had done for Naomi. Boaz always made sure Ruth and Naomi had enough to eat. And he made sure no one harmed Ruth. Soon Ruth and Boaz fell in love.

My work is amazing! Boaz and Ruth were married and had children—and one of those children was the grandfather of King David. Through this family line, My Son and your Savior, Jesus, was born.

Snuggle Session

Ruth moved away from home because she loved Naomi. Name some people you love.

_____

_____

_____

_____

God made sure Boaz was able to help take care of Ruth and Naomi. Who helps take care of you?

_____

_____

_____

_____

My Prayer

Dear God, thank You for giving me people who love me and who help You take care of me.

God's Promise

"Here is my command. Love each other, just as I have loved you." — JOHN 15:12

1 Samuel 1

Hannah Cries for a Child

WHEN I AM SAD, HELP ME TO SEEK YOU. . . .

Hannah cried and poured out her prayer before Me. She wanted a child so much. So she promised Me. . .

"O Lord, if You give me a child, I will give him back to You all the days of his life. No razor shall touch his head."

Now Eli the priest heard Hannah's plea and blessed her. And so did I. I remembered Hannah and gave her a son, Samuel.

And just as Hannah promised, when the child was old enough, she took him to Eli the priest and gave him back to Me. Samuel lived in the temple and became a great prophet of Israel.

Snuggle Session

How do you think your mommy and daddy felt when they found out you were going to be their child?

_____

_____

_____

_____

How have your parents given you back to God?

_____

_____

_____

_____

My Prayer

Thank You, God, for giving me the love of my family.

God's Promise

"He richly blesses everyone who calls on him." — ROMANS 10:12

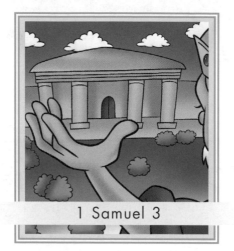

1 Samuel 3

Samuel Learns to Hear God

LORD, HELP ME TO LISTEN TO YOU. . . .

Because Hannah had given Samuel to Me, he grew up in the temple. After several years Samuel knew many things about Me, but he did not yet know how to listen to Me.

One night when the boy Samuel was sleeping, he heard someone calling, "Samuel, Samuel." He went to the old priest, Eli.

"What is it, Eli? Were you calling me?"

"No, I wasn't. Go back and lie down." Eli didn't realize that it was Me who was calling Samuel.

After Samuel went back to bed, he again heard someone calling him.

"What is it, Eli? What do you want?"

"I don't want anything. Go back and lie down," Eli said.

After the third time, Eli said, "It must be God." He was right. It was Me.

Samuel learned to hear My voice better and better. As Samuel became a man, he continued to love Me, and the people of Israel grew to admire and respect him. After Eli died, Samuel became the leader of Israel until he was a very old man.

Snuggle Session

Do you ever have a hard time listening to anyone?

_____

_____

_____

_____

What do you think it would be like to never be able
to hear anything?

_____

_____

_____

_____

My Prayer

Dear God, help me to learn to hear You.

God's Promise

"Anyone who hears my word and believes him who sent me has eternal life." — JOHN 5:22

1 Samuel 8–10

Saul Is Chosen King

LORD, NEVER LET ME STRAY FROM
YOUR DIRECTION. . . .

The people of Israel grumbled for a king to lead
their country. Samuel disagreed, but the people
wouldn't listen. I told Samuel, "I will send the people

a king, but he will be a stranger."

The next day, Saul, a handsome man, and his servant were looking for his father's lost donkeys. Tired, Saul decided to go home. "Wait," said the servant. "I have heard of a man of God in the city who can help us."

So Saul and his servant traveled to the city to meet the man of God. I had already told Samuel that Saul was coming. Samuel noticed the men coming toward him. "I am the one you are looking for," said Samuel. "Your donkeys have been found. You will eat with me today, and tomorrow I will tell you what the Lord has said."

The next morning, Samuel poured oil on Saul's head and anointed him king of Israel. "You have been chosen to lead God's people."

Snuggle Session

The Israelites asked God for a king, even after God said this was not a good idea. Have you ever done something your parents said you should not do? What happened?

_____

_____

_____

God chose Saul to lead His people. God has also chosen you to be His child. How do you think God might use you?

_____

_____

_____

My Prayer

God, help me to always work to be the person You want me to be.

God's Promise

"The Lord loves you. God chose you from the beginning." — 2 THESSALONIANS 2:13

1 Samuel 16

David Is
Anointed King

BECAUSE OF YOU, LORD,
I FEEL IMPORTANT. . . .

After I made Saul the king of Israel, he disobeyed

Me. So I told Samuel to find a new king.

"I am sending you to Jesse of Bethlehem. One of

his sons will be king," I said.

Samuel began his journey to Bethlehem just as I had commanded. He met Jesse, a man who had eight sons.

Seven of Jesse's sons were introduced to Samuel. "God has not chosen any of these sons. Do you have any others?" asked Samuel.

"Yes, my youngest son is in the fields attending the flocks," replied Jesse.

"Send for him," requested Samuel.

The youngest son, David, appeared before Samuel. "He is the chosen one," said Samuel as he anointed David in the midst of his brothers.

Who would have ever thought a young shepherd boy would rule over Israel? But that day I chose David to be the future king.

Snuggle Session

Samuel talked to God often. How can you talk to God?

_____

_____

_____

_____

When you talk to God, what do you say?

_____

_____

_____

_____

My Prayer

Thank You, God, for allowing me to talk to You through prayer!

God's Promise

"If you believe, you will receive what you ask for when you pray." — MATTHEW 21:22

1 Samuel 17–18

David and Goliath

LORD, THANK YOU FOR HELPING ME WITH
MY GREATEST BATTLES. . . .

One day the Philistines gathered their armies for
war against My people. The Philistines' champion
was a soldier named Goliath. He was over nine feet
tall, and everybody was afraid of him. . .except

David, who was still a young boy.

Every morning Goliath stood in front of the Israelites and challenged them. "Choose a man to fight me. If he kills me, the Philistines will be your servants. If I kill the man, you will be our servants!"

David heard the dare and accepted it. The Israelites begged David not to fight Goliath for fear he would be killed. But David trusted Me to keep him safe.

Everybody gathered to see the battle. Goliath laughed at the young boy. But as he neared David for attack, David took a stone from his pouch, placed it in his sling, and threw it. The stone hit Goliath on his forehead, and he died. The Israelites cheered in victory and loved David.

They loved him so much that it made King Saul very jealous.

Snuggle Session

God helped David not to be afraid of Goliath. Who helps you when you are afraid?

_____

_____

_____

David was just a boy, yet he defeated Goliath when no one else was brave enough to try. When was a time you were brave?

_____

_____

_____

My Prayer

Thank You, God, for helping me with my biggest problems.

God's Promise

"There is no one like the God of Israel. He rides in the heavens to help you." — DEUTERONOMY 33:26

1 Samuel 20

David's Best Friend

THANK YOU FOR MY FRIENDS. . . .

Jonathan was in a jam. He was David's very best

friend but also King Saul's son, and Saul wanted to

kill David. I did amazing things through David, and

the Israelites loved him. Saul's jealousy over David's

popularity drove Saul crazy.

Jonathan knew his father wanted to kill David. So he traveled to David and said, "My father wants to kill you. Guard yourself until tomorrow morning, and keep yourself well hidden. I will talk to my father, the king, for you."

When Saul found out that Jonathan had warned David, he was furious. Jonathan could see that Saul's anger was so great David would not be safe. Jonathan warned David to run away, and David escaped from Saul that night.

Snuggle Session

I love my friends because. . .

_____

_____

_____

_____

Some of the friends I love and pray for are. . .

_____

_____

_____

_____

My Prayer

Thank You, God, for all of my friends.

God's Promise

"A friend loves at all times. He is there to help when trouble comes." — PROVERBS 17:17

2 Samuel 5, 12

David Becomes King

THANK YOU, GOD, THAT YOU FORGIVE ME
WHEN I DO WRONG. . . .

After Saul died, I chose David to be the greatest

king of all the land. He followed after My own heart

and listened to My every word. I protected him in

battles and made him very rich. I gave him many talents, too. David loved to play the harp and write songs and poems. I loved him deeply.

But one time David hurt Me. David did a terrible thing. He took someone who did not belong to him. And I revealed David's sin to Nathan. Nathan was a prophet, David's adviser and friend. It was his job to tell King David he had sinned.

Scared that the king would be angry with him, Nathan went to David with a story. He told the king about a rich man who stole something valuable from a poor man.

King David became very angry and said, "How could this rich man have no pity for this poor man?"

Nathan replied, "You are the man in the story."

King David realized he had sinned, and he asked Me to forgive him. I knew how sorry he felt and forgave him.

Snuggle Session

God gave David many talents, or things that he could do well. What talents has God given you?

_____

_____

_____

_____

When I sing, I feel. . .

_____

_____

_____

_____

My Prayer

Thank You, God, for forgiving me when I ask.

God's Promise

"Forgive, and you will be forgiven."

— LUKE 6:37

1 Chronicles 29, 2 Chronicles 1–7

Solomon Becomes King

PLEASE GIVE ME WISDOM, TOO, LIKE YOU
GAVE KING SOLOMON. . . .

The time had come when King David stopped
being king and made his son Solomon the new king.
Solomon had a big job in front of him. His job was

to build My temple.

One night during a dream, I appeared to Solomon and told him to ask for whatever he wanted. Solomon didn't ask for money. Solomon didn't ask for a long life. Solomon said, "Please, Lord, give me wisdom to help lead Your people."

I was pleased by his request. I granted Solomon his desire for wisdom and also blessed him with more riches than any other king had ever known.

Solomon used his wisdom to lead My people, and he used his money to build My temple. When the temple was completed, Solomon gave it to Me. And that day I moved into the temple and told Solomon that I would be there forever.

Snuggle Session

What is the best gift you have ever received?

_____

_____

_____

_____

What is the best gift you have ever given anyone?

_____

_____

_____

_____

Solomon built a temple for God. How do you think he felt doing this wonderful thing for God?

_____

_____

_____

My Prayer

Dear God, please give me wisdom like You gave King Solomon.

God's Promise

"I know that you want truth to be in my heart. You teach me wisdom deep down inside me." — PSALM 51:6

1 Kings 17

The Widow of Zarephath

I WILL TRUST YOU ALWAYS TO TAKE
CARE OF ME. . . .

In the land of Zarephath, the crops died because it didn't rain for a very long time. The flour and oil the people needed to make bread was very expensive and hard to find. A woman and her son had just enough flour and oil to prepare one last meal. They didn't know where they would get any more food after that. One of My prophets, Elijah, traveled to the town of Zarephath and asked the widow for food.

"I'm sorry, my friend, I have no bread. I have only a handful of flour and a little oil in my jar," replied the woman.

"Do not fear, but do as you are told. I will then take care of your flour and oil. They will never run dry," said Elijah gently.

So the woman willingly shared her little bit of food with Elijah. And I filled her oil and flour containers each day. I took care of her and the boy just as Elijah had promised. The widow believed in Me!

Snuggle Session

The woman and boy in Zarephath were hungry and had only enough food for one more meal. What is the hungriest you have ever been?

_____

_____

_____

_____

My favorite meal is. . .

_____

_____

My Prayer

Dear God, I will always trust You to take care of me.

God's Promise

"Trust in him." — PSALM 4:5

1 Kings 18

Elijah's Challenge

I WILL STAND FIRM ON MY LOVE
FOR YOU, GOD. . . .

Well, the big showdown finally arrived. Elijah, my
prophet, lived in Israel in a time when many people
prayed to a god who wasn't even real: Baal. Elijah
challenged the evil King Ahab and Baal's prophets to

a competition to prove I was real and Baal was not.

Elijah told them, "I am the only one of God's prophets left. Baal has 450 prophets. You make a sacrifice and call to Baal. I will call on the real God. The one who answers by lighting the sacrifice on fire is the real God."

All day long Baal's prophets shouted and danced and prayed but received no answer. Elijah teased them: "Shout louder! Maybe your god is sleeping!"

Then the time came when it was Elijah's turn. After pouring water on his sacrifice, Elijah called on the one true God. Fire exploded from the sky, and I destroyed the sacrifice.

All the people fell on their faces and yelled, "The Lord, He is God!" Elijah seized the prophets of Baal, and not one survived.

Snuggle Session

Many people were angry at Elijah for saying that Baal wasn't real. How do you feel when people are angry at you?

_____

_____

_____

Elijah was very brave to stand up for God when others said God wasn't real. When is a time you have been brave?

_____

_____

_____

My Prayer

Dear God, I will stand firm in my love for You.

God's Promise

"If you do not stand firm in your faith, you will not stand at all." — ISAIAH 7:9

2 Kings 2

Elisha Carries On

BLESS ME WITH YOUR SPIRIT, LORD. . . .

Elisha loved his friend Elijah and followed him everywhere. But Elijah knew he would soon be leaving to join Me in heaven. I called Elisha to carry on in Elijah's place.

"Soon I will be leaving, my friend," explained

Elijah. "You will have to stay here. Please let me know what I can do for you before I leave."

Saddened by the news, Elisha asked to be allowed to continue Elijah's ministry. He did this by saying, "I want a double portion of your spirit upon me."

"Elisha, you have asked a difficult thing, but if you see me when I leave, it will be given to you," responded Elijah. Just then, horses made of fire pulling a chariot of fire exploded through the sky, swept down from heaven, and took Elijah away. Elisha saw it.

Tears filled Elisha's eyes, but I blessed him with the double portion of My Spirit, the same Spirit that had filled Elijah. Elisha became an awesome prophet who performed many miracles and healed the sick.

Snuggle Session

Elisha knew Elijah was going to leave. How do you feel when someone you love leaves?

_____

_____

_____

_____

What do you think it would feel like to ride in a chariot of fire?

_____

_____

_____

_____

My Prayer

Dear God, please bless me with Your spirit.

God's Promise

"I will pour out my Spirit on your children."

— ISAIAH 44:3

Nehemiah 1–2, 4, 6

Rebuilding the Walls

SHOW ME WHAT I CAN DO TO HELP MAKE
THINGS BETTER, THE WAY NEHEMIAH DID. . . .

The Israelites were very sad. The Babylonians had
captured them. They had taken the Israelites away
from their homes and from their cities, including the
city of Jerusalem where My temple was. For many
years they lived in the country of Babylon. One day

news arrived in the palace in Babylon: Jerusalem had been destroyed. The king's cupbearer, My prophet Nehemiah, cried for days. He could not hide his sorrow from the king.

Nehemiah begged the king saying, "If I have found favor in your eyes, let me return to Jerusalem to rebuild the city." The king allowed Nehemiah to return to Jerusalem. I also moved the king's heart so that he allowed Nehemiah to use Babylon's materials to rebuild the city.

Nehemiah was a man of strength and leadership. He depended on Me. Together with the help of many people, Nehemiah began rebuilding the walls. When Israel's enemies heard what they were doing, they threatened to come and attack the Israelites. Finally Nehemiah and the Israelites finished rebuilding the walls around Jerusalem in just fifty-two days. Because they finished such a big job so quickly, Israel's enemies became very afraid. They realized God was helping the Israelites rebuild the city.

Snuggle Session

Nehemiah helped rebuild the walls of Jerusalem. How do you think he rebuilt those walls?

_____

_____

_____

_____

When something breaks, I feel. . .

_____

_____

_____

_____

My Prayer

Dear God, show me what I can do to help make things better, the way Nehemiah did.

God's Promise

"The Lord is a place of safety for those who have been beaten down. He keeps them safe in times of trouble."

— PSALM 9:9

Esther 3, 7

Esther Saves the Israelites

KEEP ME SAFE FROM MY ENEMIES. . . .

More troubles came to My people, the Hebrews.
They were about to be killed at the evil hands of
Haman, the Persian king's highest commander. It all
started when a Hebrew named Mordecai would not

worship Haman. He worshiped only Me. This made Haman very angry. Haman decided he wanted to kill all of the Hebrews.

So he went to the king and lied. "King, there are people in your kingdom who do not obey your laws. I ask that they be killed."

After hearing Haman's plea, the king agreed. But unknown to him, his wife, Queen Esther, was also a Hebrew. She was Mordecai's cousin. She knew her life was in danger, but with the help of Mordecai, she prepared a plan.

She invited Haman to attend a banquet with her and the king. During the feast she announced to the king that she would soon be killed along with all her people.

The king asked, "Who would do such a thing?"

Queen Esther replied, "Your evil servant Haman."

This news made King Xerxes furious, and Haman died instead of the Hebrews.

Snuggle Session

Esther and the Hebrews were worried about what the king would do. Have you ever been worried?

_____

_____

_____

_____

When do you feel the safest?

_____

_____

_____

_____

My Prayer

Dear God, keep me safe from my enemies.

God's Promise

"When I'm in trouble, he will keep me safe in his house." — PSALM 27:5

Job 1–2, 42

Job Remains Faithful

HELP ME TO BE FAITHFUL, LORD,
IN ALL I DO. . . .

Satan challenged My servant Job, and disaster fell

upon him. But I knew Job would remain faithful. Job

lost everything he owned—his livestock, servants,

sons, and daughters.

Job thought his life couldn't get any worse, but it did. His body was covered with painful sores. All his friends and even his wife thought Job had done something awful to deserve such punishment. But he hadn't.

"What have you done to have caused this much suffering?" they asked.

But I knew Job's heart. I loved him. Job continued to give praise and glory to Me, and at the end of his trouble, I returned his wealth, his family, and doubled his blessings!

Snuggle Session

What's the most important thing you have ever lost?

_____

_____

_____

_____

When I lose something special, I feel. . .

_____

_____

_____

_____

My Prayer

Dear God, help me be faithful in all I do.

God's Promise

"Lord, to those who are faithful you show that you are faithful." — PSALM 18:25

Isaiah 1–2, 9, 11, 32, 56

The Prophet Isaiah

THANK YOU FOR THE GIFTS YOU
HAVE GIVEN ME. . . .

I gave Isaiah many gifts. First of all, he was one

of My prophets. He foretold the future of Israel and

Judah, and of the coming of Jesus. Isaiah was a poet

and a preacher; he was a leader of his people, and he taught them about Me. Because Isaiah had all these wonderful gifts, I chose him to give a message to the Israelites: Everyone needs cleansing from their sins; everyone needs My forgiving grace.

Soon, I promised, I would be sending My Son.

Snuggle Session

God gave Isaiah many gifts. Why is it fun to give gifts?

_____

_____

_____

_____

God helped Isaiah know what would happen in the future. If you could see what was going to happen tomorrow, what do you think you'd see?

_____

_____

_____

_____

My Prayer

Dear God, thank You for the gifts You have given me.

God's Promise

"How much more will your Father who is in heaven give good gifts to those who ask him!"

— MATTHEW 7:11

Jeremiah 1, 7, 52

The Prophet Jeremiah

HELP ME TO SHOW COMPASSION
TO OTHERS. . . .

I gave my prophet Jeremiah a difficult job. I sent
him to tell the Israelites the punishment for their sin. It
was not a fun job. The people ignored him and were

not sorry about the wrong things they were doing. Jeremiah felt so bad that he cried over the pain and sorrow of his people.

The events I told Jeremiah did happen. And Jeremiah, "the weeping prophet," continued to feel sorry for the Israelites through all the long years of their suffering.

Snuggle Session

Jeremiah had to do a hard job for God. Is hard work any fun?

_____

_____

_____

_____

I cry when. . .

_____

_____

_____

_____

My Prayer

Dear God, help me to show people I care about them.

God's Promise

"He takes good care of those who trust in him." — NAHUM 1:7

Jeremiah 18

Jeremiah at the Potter's House

HELP ME TO OBEY YOU. . . .

I told Jeremiah to go to the potter's house to receive

the message I had for him. When Jeremiah arrived,

the potter was making a pot on a pottery wheel.

Jeremiah watched the man. When the pot he was making turned out to be no good, he rolled the clay into a ball and started over.

I told Jeremiah, "This is what I want you to say to the Israelites: This is why the Israelites need to listen to Me. Just like the potter can make the clay become anything he desires, so I can make the Israelites anything I desire. If I tell the Israelites I am going to do a good thing for them, but then they do wrong things, I will change My mind. I will not do the good thing I had planned. And if I say I am going to discipline them, but they ask for forgiveness, then I will forgive them. I will not discipline them."

When Jeremiah told the people what I said, they became angry with him and threatened to kill him. But I protected Jeremiah.

Snuggle Session

You are like a soft piece of clay or Play-Doh to God; He can make you into many wonderful things. How do you think God might form you or make you as you grow?

_____

_____

_____

_____

What would you like to be when you grow up?

_____

_____

_____

_____

My Prayer

Help me to obey You, God, and let You make me into something wonderful.

God's Promise

"Blessed are all those who go to him for safety." — PSALM 2:12

Daniel 3

The Fiery Furnace

I WILL ALWAYS WORSHIP YOU. . . .

Because my people did not listen to the prophets,
I allowed them to be captured and taken to Babylon.
Nebuchadnezzar was the king of this land, and
some people had broken his law. Punishment for not
worshiping his idol meant being thrown into a fiery

furnace. Three men—Shadrach, Meshach, and
Abednego—refused to bow down to the king's idol.
I was proud of them.

"Bring the men to me," demanded the king. When
the three Hebrew men stood before him, he asked
them, "Is it true that you do not worship my gods?"

"We will not serve your gods, and we will not worship your idols. We will only worship our own God,"
replied the men.

"Cast them into the burning furnace!" commanded
the king.

But I protected them. They remained unharmed in
the middle of the fire!

"No other God can save people that way! Never
again will I allow anyone to say anything bad about
your God," said the king.

Snuggle Session

How do you think God feels when we do what is right?

_____

_____

_____

_____

What do you think of when you see a fire?

_____

_____

_____

_____

My Prayer

Thank You, God, for protecting me.

God's Promise

"*He will not desert those who are faithful to him. They will be kept safe forever.*"

— PSALM 37:28

Handwriting on the Wall

GOD, YOU ARE WISE BEYOND WORDS. . . .

One night, while the Israelites were still slaves in Babylon, the king was having a big party at his house. During the party, something mysterious happened. The fingers of a hand appeared and started writing something on the wall. As the king watched the hand write, he was so terrified he fell down.

Later, the king sent for his magicians and all his wisest people. He wanted them to tell him what the message on the wall said. The king said, "Whoever

can read this message and tell
me what it means will become
one of the most powerful men
in my kingdom."

However, none of the king's men could read the
message on the wall. The queen came to him and
said, "There is a man in your kingdom who can tell
what dreams mean. He can explain riddles and hard
problems. Send for him. He will tell you what the writing means."

So the king sent for Daniel. Daniel read the message, and in it I told the king that he was about to
die. I said that the king hadn't obeyed Me, and so I
was going to give his kingdom to someone else. I pro-
vided Daniel the wisdom to interpret the mysteries so
people would know that I am God.

Snuggle Session

God was able to give Daniel the wisdom to tell the king what the writing on the wall meant. How do you think God gives you wisdom?

_____

_____

_____

_____

What do you think you are really good at or that God has given you a talent to do?

_____

_____

_____

My Prayer

Give me wisdom, God, to know what You want me to know and to let You teach me new things.

God's Promise

"He is the Lord of kings. He explains mysteries." — DANIEL 2:47

Daniel 6

Daniel Is Thrown to the Lions

LORD, THANK YOU FOR SAVING ME. . . .

My people had other problems in Babylon.
Because they were jealous, King Darius's officials
found fault with Daniel, the mighty prophet who had
risen to power under the king.

The evil men plotted against Daniel and asked the king to enforce a new law. The law stated that anyone who prayed to any god or man except the king should be thrown into the lions' den.

Knowing the new law, Daniel continued to bow down to Me, not once but three times a day.

Upset, the king said, "Throw him to the lions! And, Daniel, may the God you chose to serve save you!"

That night the king could not sleep or eat because he was worried about Daniel. The next morning he rushed to the lions' den. "Daniel!" he cried out. "Has your God saved you?"

Of course I saved him! I closed the lions' mouths and protected Daniel. "King Darius, live forever," said Daniel.

The king was overjoyed and believed in Me. Then he threw the evil men who accused Daniel into the lions' den. And on that day, the lions were very hungry!

Snuggle Session

Daniel prayed to God because he loved Him. Why do you pray to God?

_____

_____

_____

_____

I pray to God when. . .

_____

_____

_____

_____

My Prayer

Dear God, thank You for saving me.

God's Promise

"Everyone who calls out to me will be saved."

— JOEL 2:32

Jonah 1–2

Jonah Flees from God

HELP ME TO OBEY YOU, LORD. . . .

And then there was Jonah. I told Jonah to go to the great city of Nineveh, the capital of the mighty Assyrian Empire.

"I am not going to Nineveh," said Jonah. And he

ran away and boarded a ship traveling in the opposite direction.

I caused a terrifying storm. And while the sea roared, Jonah slept in a bunk below the deck.

"Who has caused this great storm?" asked the sailors.

Jonah woke up. He realized he had caused the storm because he didn't listen to Me. "Throw me overboard," he said, "and the storm will end."

So the sailors tossed Jonah overboard, and he began to sink.

But I was merciful. A big fish swallowed Jonah. While in the belly of the fish, Jonah told Me he was sorry. I loved Jonah and forgave him.

But I told Jonah to finish his job. So he went to Nineveh to preach My message. "Repent from your evil ways and return to Me or I will destroy your city in forty days."

They listened to My message and returned to Me. Their city was saved.

Snuggle Session

Jonah had a problem obeying God the first time. Just like Jonah had to obey God, you have to obey your parents. Why is it important to obey your parents?

_____

_____

_____

_____

I obey my parents because. . .

_____

_____

_____

_____

My Prayer

Dear God, sometimes obeying is hard. Help me to do what You ask of me.

God's Promise

"Go to the great city of Nineveh. Preach against it. The sins of its people have come to my attention. But Jonah ran away from the Lord." — JONAH 1:2-3

Luke 1

John the Baptist Is Born

THANK YOU FOR YOUR BLESSINGS, GOD. . . .

This was the day Zechariah had been waiting for.
As one of My priests, he had been chosen to enter the
holiest place in the temple and honor Me. But when
Zechariah entered the holy place, Gabriel, one of

my angels, met him there.

Zechariah shook with fear. Gabriel said to him, "Don't be afraid. I am here to tell you that you and your wife, Elizabeth, are going to have a special baby. You are to name him John. John will grow up and tell people about God's Son."

Zechariah didn't believe Gabriel. He said, "How can this be? My wife and I are too old to have children."

Gabriel replied, "God Himself sent me to give you this news. And because you do not believe, you will not be able to speak from now until the baby is born."

Soon Elizabeth became pregnant and praised God for her baby. When the baby was born, all the neighbors and relatives wanted to name the baby after his father. Zechariah, who still couldn't talk, wrote, "His name is John." Immediately God opened his mouth, and he was able to speak again.

Snuggle Session

How do you think your parents felt when they found out that you were their special child?

_____

_____

_____

_____

Zechariah was very faithful to God, but he had a difficult time believing that his wife would have a baby because of how old they were; in the end Zechariah learned that God can do anything. What has God done for you?

_____

_____

_____

_____

My Prayer

Thank You, God, for being the God who can do all things. I trust You with my life and want to do what will please You.

God's Promise

"If you believe, you will receive what you ask for when you pray." — MATTHEW 21:22

Luke 1

Blessed among Women

JESUS, THANK YOU FOR YOUR
WONDERFUL LOVE. . . .

The time had come for Me to send My Good News
to the earth. So I sent My angel Gabriel to a girl
named Mary, and he spoke these words: "You will
give birth to a Son. You must name Him Jesus. He will

be great and will be called the Son of the Most High God."

"How can this be?" asked Mary. "I'm not married yet."

However, Mary believed the angel and praised My name. She quickly left to visit her cousin Elizabeth to tell her the news.

Now Elizabeth was going to have a baby, too, and when she heard Mary's voice, the baby leaped inside her. "God has blessed you more than other women," said Elizabeth with joy. She already knew the plans I had for Mary.

But when Joseph, the man who was to take Mary as his bride, found out about the news, he decided not to marry her.

One night in a dream, I sent Gabriel again, and he appeared to Joseph. "Joseph, do not be afraid to take Mary as your wife. The child she is carrying is the Son of God. And you will name him Jesus." And so they were married.

Snuggle Session

The angel Gabriel visited Mary and told her she was going to have a baby. What do you think Gabriel looked like?

_____

_____

_____

_____

When I dream, I dream about. . .

_____

_____

_____

_____

My Prayer

Thank You, God, for Your wonderful love.

God's Promise

"The angel said to her, 'Do not be afraid, Mary. God is very pleased with you. You will become pregnant and give birth to a son. You must name him Jesus.'"

— LUKE 1:30-31

Luke 2

The Time Is Near

JESUS, THANK YOU FOR THE LIFE
YOU GAVE ME. . . .

The time drew near for My Son to be born. But
before Jesus arrived in this world, Joseph and Mary
traveled to their homeland, Bethlehem, because the
government wanted to count everyone in the whole

land. Everywhere people filled the city.

Mary needed to rest, but each and every inn was full. At last, Mary and Joseph found comfort in an old dusty stable where the animals slept. During this time, Mary's baby Son entered the world. She wrapped Him in cloths and laid Him in the animals' drinking trough.

And the words from My prophets were fulfilled: "For there is born to you this day in the city of David, a Savior, who is Christ the Lord."

Shepherds from a nearby field heard about the Child from an angel. They, too, came to worship the newborn King, Jesus.

Snuggle Session

A stable is a home for many animals. What do you think Mary, Joseph, and Jesus saw and smelled in their stable?

_____

_____

_____

_____

Christmas is Jesus' birthday. How can you help celebrate that day?

_____

_____

_____

My Prayer

Jesus, thank You for the life You give me.

God's Promise

"While Joseph and Mary were there, the time came for the child to be born. She gave birth to her first baby. It was a boy. She wrapped him in large strips of cloth. Then she placed him in a manger. There was no room for them in the inn."

— LUKE 2:6–7

Luke 2

Anna and Simeon Wait for the Lord

LORD, TEACH ME TO WAIT FOR YOU. . . .

Several of My people waited a very long time to see Jesus. Anna and Simeon had served Me for years. Anna prayed and fasted faithfully in the temple. She longed for the birth of the Savior. When she saw Jesus, she knew He was the Messiah. Anna did not keep this joyous news to herself but made it known to all who would listen.

And Simeon, well, I told him that he would not die until he saw the Savior of the world. The Holy Spirit moved him when he went to the temple, and he recognized My Son, Jesus. He took Jesus in his arms and praised Me for him. Joseph and Mary marveled at the fact that Simeon already knew that Jesus was the Christ Child.

Snuggle Session

Anna and Simeon had to wait for the birth of Jesus.
Sometimes it can be difficult to wait. Why is waiting
sometimes hard?

_____

_____

_____

_____

One thing I have waited for is. . .

_____

_____

_____

_____

My Prayer

Lord, teach me to wait for You, even when I don't feel like it.

God's Promise

"Anna came up to Jesus' family at that very moment. She gave thanks to God. And she spoke about the child to all who were looking forward to the time when Jerusalem would be set free." — LUKE 2:38

Matthew 2

The Wise Men

HELP ME TO FOLLOW YOUR LIGHT. . . .

After the birth of My Son, Jesus, three wise men
from the east saw a beautiful, bright star and followed
it to Bethlehem. They heard about the news and traveled to worship the new King.

When they got near Bethlehem, they went to King

Herod of Judah. They asked Herod, "Where is the Child who has been born to be King of the Jews? We have come to worship him." When Herod heard this, he was very upset. He was the leader, and he didn't want anyone around who claimed to be a king.

"Find this new King and tell me where I can worship Him, too," lied King Herod. He really wanted to know where Jesus was so he could kill the Child.

The wise men agreed to find the baby King, and they continued to follow the star. Finally, they bowed down and worshiped Jesus and brought Him many gifts of gold, myrrh, and incense.

Now, I warned the wise men in a dream not to return to King Herod. So they listened and returned home by a different route. This made King Herod furious!

Snuggle Session

The wise men worshiped Jesus and gave Him special gifts. What special gift could you give Jesus?

_____

_____

_____

_____

What is a special gift you have received from someone who loves you?

_____

_____

_____

_____

My Prayer

Help me to follow Your light, God.

God's Promise

"The Wise Men went to the house. There they saw the child with his mother Mary. They bowed down and worshiped him. Then they opened their treasures. They gave him gold, incense and myrrh."

— MATTHEW 2:11

John 1, Mark 1, Luke 3

John the Baptist

LORD, FORGIVE ME WHEN I DO WRONG. . . .

John the Baptist was Jesus' cousin, the son of
Zechariah and Elizabeth. I chose John to prepare the
way for Jesus. John preached in the wilderness of
Judea: "Repent, for the kingdom of heaven is near!"
People traveled from all over that area to hear

John speak of the coming of My Son. He baptized the people who confessed their sins. His message was clear. He said: "I baptize you with water, but the One who comes after me will baptize you with the Holy Spirit and fire."

One day Jesus traveled to the place where John was preaching and asked John to baptize Him. "I am not worthy to carry Your sandals. You should baptize me!" said John.

But Jesus insisted, and so John agreed and baptized Him in the Jordan River. As Jesus came out of the water, a great light shone down from heaven. My Spirit, like a beautiful dove, flew down and landed on Jesus. All the people standing there heard My voice from heaven say: "This is My Son whom I love, and I am pleased with Him."

Snuggle Session

Wouldn't it have been great to see God's signs from heaven when Jesus was baptized? How would you have felt if you had seen God's Spirit and heard His voice?

_____

_____

_____

_____

What do you think heaven will be like?

_____

_____

_____

My Prayer

Lord, thank You for your forgiveness when I do wrong.

God's Promise

"Jesus was coming up out of the water. Just then he saw heaven being torn open. He saw the Holy Spirit coming down on him like a dove. A voice spoke to him from heaven. It said, 'You are my Son, and I love you. I am very pleased with you.'"

— MARK 1:10-11

Matthew 4

Peter Follows Jesus

LET ME TELL OTHERS ABOUT
THE GOOD NEWS. . . .

One day My Son, Jesus, met a man named Peter

and his brother Andrew as they were fishing. He said,

"Follow Me, and I will make you fishers of men."

Immediately Peter and Andrew dropped their nets and followed Him. They believed Jesus and became two of His twelve disciples. The other disciples' names were: James, John, Philip, Bartholomew, Matthew, Thomas, James (the son of Alphaeus), Thaddaeus, Simon the Zealot, and Judas. Throughout the land, they preached Jesus' messages.

But one time Jesus told Peter he would fail Him. Peter believed he would never fail Jesus, and he said so. But later Peter did fail Jesus. He lied about knowing Jesus three times! But Jesus forgave him and continued to love His friend.

Peter's faith grew, and he never gave up preaching My message.

Snuggle Session

Peter acted like he didn't know Jesus—three times!
How would you feel if one of your best friends denied
knowing you?

_____

_____

_____

Have you ever known someone who other people
didn't want to be around? How do you think that
makes the person feel?

_____

_____

_____

I must tell others about Jesus because. . .

_____

_____

_____

My Prayer

Help me, God, to tell others the good news about
Your Son.

God's Promise

" 'Come. Follow me,' Jesus said. 'I will make
you fishers of people.' " — MATTHEW 4:19

Luke 10

Martha Prepares a Dinner

LORD, TEACH ME WHAT IS IMPORTANT
IN MY LIFE. . . .

Busy Martha hurried around preparing a dinner for
Jesus and His friends. She got upset when her sister,
Mary, would not help her serve Jesus. Instead, Mary

sat by Jesus and listened to Him.

"Jesus, do You not care that my sister won't help me serve dinner? Tell her to help me," complained Martha.

"Martha, you are worried and upset about a lot of things. But there's only one thing that is important, and Mary knows that is listening to Me."

Jesus knew Martha loved and served Him. But He gently reminded her that Mary chose what was most important: to sit and listen to His words.

Snuggle Session

Martha was upset because she had to work alone. Have you ever had to clean up alone? How did that make you feel?

_____

_____

_____

_____

Sometimes I feel angry when. . .

_____

_____

_____

_____

My Prayer

Lord, teach me what is important in my life.

God's Promise

" 'Martha, Martha,' the Lord answered. 'You are worried and upset about many things. But only one thing is needed. Mary has chosen what is better. And it will not be taken away from her.' "

— LUKE 10:41–42

John 1–3

The Savior of the World

THANK YOU, JESUS, FOR GIVING YOUR
LIFE TO US. . . .

Jesus is My powerful Son. He lived in heaven and
then came to the earth to fulfill my promise that whoever believes in Him will have eternal life. Even

though Jesus performed miracles showing My power, many did not believe in Him. Some people thought when My Son came to live on earth he would be the leader of an army. But Jesus didn't lead an army. So, many didn't believe He was My Son.

But others did believe the promises of Jesus. Those people will be with Me forever. I call everyone who believes in Jesus "My children." Each time people believed in Jesus, their spirits began to live that day.

But Jesus didn't come only for the people who were alive on earth when He was here. He came for everybody. He came for you, too. I want you to live forever with Him.

Snuggle Session

Jesus came to earth to help everyone. He would have come even if you were the only one on earth that He could help. How much do you think Jesus loves you?

_____

_____

_____

_____

Jesus loves me because. . .

_____

_____

_____

_____

My Prayer

Thank You, God, for giving Your Son for me so I can live with You forever.

God's Promise

"God loved the world so much that he gave his one and only Son. Anyone who believes in him will not die but will have eternal life."

— JOHN 3:16

John 2

Jesus' First Miracle

LORD, HELP ME TO OBEY
YOUR INSTRUCTIONS. . . .

My Son, Jesus, His disciples, and His mother,
Mary, attended a huge wedding. Beauty and joy
filled the room. But then the wedding guests ran

into a small problem. The wine was all gone. People started to mutter and complain. This worried Mary.

"What do you want Me to do about it?" asked Jesus.

But Mary knew her Son could take care of it. And He did.

Next to Him stood six huge containers. "Fill the containers with water," Jesus told the people around Him. So the people filled the containers all the way to the top.

"Now, take a cup, dip it in the jar, and take it to your master," said Jesus. The master didn't know where the cup had come from, but when he drank from it, he said it held the best wine he had ever tasted. Everybody was amazed.

This was Jesus' first miracle, and it showed many people how powerful He was.

Snuggle Session

Jesus could perform miracles. He was amazing! When the guests saw Jesus' miracle, they probably felt _____. Why do you think they felt that way?

_____

_____

_____

_____

I see Jesus' miracles in. . .

_____

_____

_____

My Prayer

Lord, thank You for Your wonderful miracles that You show me everyday!

God's Promise

"In loud voices they praised him for all the miracles they had seen." — LUKE 19:37

Matthew 14

Jesus Feeds the People

THANK YOU, JESUS, FOR TAKING CARE
OF ALL MY NEEDS. . . .

Crowds loved to hear Jesus speak. They followed
Him everywhere. One day near the Sea of Galilee,
Jesus spent all His time healing the sick and preaching

My words. However, it was getting dark, and the crowd became hungry.

"Lord, send the people away so they can go eat," said the disciples.

Jesus replied, "They do not need to leave. You give them something to eat."

"But we only have five loaves of bread and two fish," they answered. "How can we feed all these people?"

"Bring the food to Me," said Jesus. He took the food and lifted it to heaven and gave thanks to Me. "Give this food to the people."

The disciples began passing out food to everyone who was there. They kept passing it out until everyone had eaten all they wanted. There was enough food for everyone! That day Jesus fed about five thousand men, besides all the women and children.

Snuggle Session

Jesus used a small amount of food to feed many people. How do you think He did it?

_____

_____

_____

_____

My favorite food is. . .

_____

_____

_____

_____

My Prayer

Thank You, Jesus, for taking care of all my needs.

God's Promise

"Then Jesus directed the people to sit down on the grass. He took the five loaves and the two fish. He looked up to heaven and gave thanks. He broke the loaves into pieces. Then he gave them to the disciples. And the disciples gave them to the people."

— MATTHEW 14:19

Jesus Walks on Water

O GOD, YOU ARE AMAZING. . . .

After Jesus had fed all the people with just five loaves of bread and two fish, He told His disciples to prepare to leave. They all got into a boat to go to a town on the other side of the sea. Jesus told them, "Go on ahead, I'll meet you later." So the disciples set out by boat across the water, and Jesus went to pray.

When evening came, Jesus was alone on the seashore. He could see His friends on the water.

They were struggling to row their boat because the wind was very strong. When it was nearly morning, Jesus set out across the water walking to them!

When Jesus' friends saw Him coming across the water, they thought He was a ghost and they were afraid. Jesus said to them, "Be brave! It is I. Don't be afraid." Then He climbed into the boat and finished riding across the sea with them.

Snuggle Session

The disciples were afraid when they saw Jesus walking on the water. He told them to be brave. How does Jesus help us to be brave?

_____

_____

_____

_____

When have you had to be brave?

_____

_____

_____

_____

My Prayer

Sometimes things scare me and I'm so glad that You help me to be brave. Thanks for loving me and taking care of all my fear.

God's Promise

"Don't be afraid. Just believe."

— MARK 5:36

Mark 4

Jesus Calms the Storm

THANK YOU, LORD, THAT YOU ALWAYS
CARE FOR ME. . . .

Tired after talking to the crowds all day, Jesus
wanted to take a boat across the lake to the other
side and rest. His disciples agreed. They left the

crowd and sailed off. While Jesus was sleeping in the boat, a terrible storm came up, knocking their boat against the waves. The little boat was about to sink.

"Teacher, wake up," the disciples screamed. "Don't You care that we are going to drown?"

Jesus stood up and scolded the wind and waves. "Quiet! Be still!" He said. And the storm died down. Soon the weather was completely calm. Then Jesus asked His disciples, "Why are you so afraid? Do you have no faith?"

Terrified, the disciples asked each other, "Who is this? Even the wind and the waves obey Him!"

Snuggle Session

How do you feel when it is stormy outside?

_____

_____

_____

_____

If you could make the weather tomorrow anything you wanted it to be, what would it be like?

_____

_____

_____

_____

My Prayer

Please be with me, God, on stormy days and nights.
I trust You to keep me safe.

God's Promise

"The earth belongs to the Lord. And so
does everything in it." — PSALM 24:1

Luke 5

A Man Learns to Walk

THANK YOU FOR FRIENDS. . . .

One day Jesus was in a house teaching. Some men brought a friend with them. They carried their friend on a mat because he couldn't walk. They wanted Jesus to heal him. But there was a big crowd around the house, and the men could not get close enough to ask Jesus to heal their friend.

So the men took their friend to the roof of the house. They removed some tiles from the roof and lowered their friend into the house right in front of Jesus! When Jesus saw how much they believed in Him, he said, "Friend, your sins are forgiven."

When the religious leaders heard Him tell the man he was forgiven, they became angry. They thought, "Only God can forgive sin."

Jesus knew what the leaders were thinking. He said, "Is it easier for me to tell this man his sin is forgiven, or to make him able to walk?" Of course anyone can say whatever he or she wants, so Jesus said, "I'm going to heal this man so you know I have God's power to do more than just talk." Then He told the man, "Get up. Take your mat and go home." Immediately the man got up and walked home, praising God. And everyone was amazed at Jesus' miracle.

Snuggle Session

Jesus was able to do miracles because He was God's Son. How would you feel if you saw Jesus work a miracle?

_____

_____

_____

_____

The crippled man had wonderful friends. They worked very hard to bring him before Jesus, and they believed that Jesus would heal their friend. Do you have good friends? Why is it important for us to have friends? Who are some of your friends?

_____

_____

_____

_____

My Prayer

Friends are a wonderful gift that You have given me, God, and I'm thankful for all of my friends. Help me be a good friend and show others that I love You.

God's Promise

"He laughs at proud people who make fun of others. But he gives grace to those who are not proud." — PROVERBS 3:34

A Visitor at Night

THANK YOU FOR FORGIVING SIN. . . .

Every time Jesus taught people about Me, the religious leaders became angry. Jesus was telling people things about Me that even the leaders didn't know. The leaders didn't believe Jesus was My Son, so when He forgave people's sins, they believed He was doing something wrong.

But one night when it was dark, a religious leader named Nicodemus came to Jesus. He said, "Teacher,

I know You are from God because of all the miracu-
lous signs You do."

Jesus answered by saying, "No one can see
heaven unless he is born again."

Nicodemus didn't understand. "How can someone
be born twice?" he asked.

Jesus explained, "Your
body gets born, and later
your spirit gets born when
you believe in Me."

Snuggle Session

When Jesus talked to Nicodemus about being born again, He was telling him that he had to have Jesus in his heart if he was going to go to heaven to see God. How does it feel to have Jesus in your heart?

_____

_____

_____

Jesus was talking to Nicodemus about how to see heaven. Jesus told him that he must be born of the body, then of the Spirit. You have been born of the body, but have you been born of the Spirit? Have you asked God to come and live in your heart?

_____

_____

_____

_____

My Prayer

God, thank You for loving me so much that You sent Jesus. I'm so glad that I have a way to know You and see You in heaven.

God's Promise

"Call out to me. I will answer you. I will tell you great things you do not know."

— JEREMIAH 33:3

Matthew, Mark, Luke, John

Jesus Teaches How to Live:
The Parables

HELP ME, GOD, TO UNDERSTAND
YOUR KINGDOM. . . .

212

Jesus and His disciples went throughout the land

preaching and teaching My message. I sent Him to

teach the crowds to love their enemies. He taught people

to forgive. He taught them not to judge others, to be the light of the earth, and to believe in Him.

Jesus loved the people and wanted to save them.

He announced, "I am the Way, the Truth, and the Life."

Sometimes Jesus would teach about heaven so the people would understand Him. He used stories called "parables" to explain My kingdom. . . .

THE MUSTARD SEED PARABLE

"The kingdom of heaven is like a mustard seed," said Jesus. "Although it is the smallest of seeds, when it grows up, it becomes the largest plant in the garden and becomes a tree. The branches reach out for the birds to make their nests."

THE WEDDING BANQUET PARABLE

Jesus explained, "The kingdom of heaven is like a king who gave a wedding party to his son. He invited very important people to the party. But the important people ignored the invitation and did not come. So the king invited the poor, the blind, and the crippled and filled the party room full of people." And Jesus said, "Many are invited, but few are chosen."

THE LOST SHEEP AND PRODIGAL SON PARABLES

"Suppose one of you has a hundred sheep," Jesus said to the sinners, "and you lose one. You will leave all the other sheep to find the lost one. It is the same in heaven, when one sinner who was lost is found. There will be great rejoicing!"

Jesus continued, "There was a man who had two

sons. The younger son demanded that his father give him his inheritance. Then the son traveled off to a distant land and spent all his money. The older son stayed with his father and worked hard for him.

When the younger son ran out of money and was hungry, he decided to go home. His father welcomed him back with open arms and gave him a big party. The older son got angry. But the father explained to the older one, "Your brother was lost, but now he is found. Let's rejoice!"

Snuggle Session

Jesus liked to tell stories. What is your favorite story?

_____

_____

_____

_____

Jesus told a story about a man who had a party and no one came. What is the best party you have ever been to?

_____

_____

_____

_____

My Prayer

Dear God, thank You for wanting everyone to hear Your good news.

God's Promise

"Go into all the world. Preach the good news to everyone." — MARK 16:15

John 11

Jesus Heals Many Lives

THANK YOU, LORD, THAT YOU MAKE
ME WHOLE. . . .

Throughout the land Jesus healed many sick
people. He made the blind able to see. He made the
deaf able to hear. He made the crippled able to walk.

And He sent evil spirits away from the people they tormented. This helped many people believe that Jesus was really My Son.

But to others, Jesus was a serious problem. The religious leaders thought My people would no longer listen to them. They wanted to stop Jesus. They began to plan how they would stop Him.

Snuggle Session

What's the sneakiest thing you have ever done?

_____

_____

_____

_____

Talk about a time when someone was mean to you.

_____

_____

_____

_____

My Prayer

Thank You, God, for caring about everyone.

God's Promise

"Anything you did for one of the least important of these brothers of mine, you did for me." — MATTHEW 25:40

Lazarus. . . Come Forth

I AM SO GLAD, DEAR LORD, THAT YOU ARE
MORE POWERFUL THAN DEATH. . . .

One of Jesus' best friends was Lazarus, Mary and Martha's brother. One day Lazarus became sick. Jesus heard the news, and He knew that Lazarus would die. He traveled back to the home of Mary and Martha to comfort them.

By the time Jesus got near Mary and Martha's home, Lazarus had died. Martha met Jesus before He got to her house. "If only You were here, Lazarus wouldn't have died," she said.

Jesus said, "Didn't I tell you that if you believed you would see God's miracles?"

"Yes," she answered. "I believe You are the Son of God, and the One who will save the world."

Jesus said, "Show me where you've put Lazarus." They showed Him the tomb; Jesus was sad and He cried. With Martha by His side, He told some men to remove the stone from in front of the tomb.

Jesus looked at Martha. "Didn't I say that if you would believe you would see the glory of God? Lazarus, come out of there!"

Lazarus did come out! He came back from the dead! After this miracle, many believed Jesus was truly My Son.

Snuggle Session

What's the most sick you have ever been?

_____

_____

_____

_____

How can we help others who are sick?

_____

_____

_____

_____

My Prayer

Dear God, thank You for Your great power and Your miracles.

God's Promise

Jesus said to them, "I have shown you many miracles from the Father."

— JOHN 10:32

Mark 12

The Widow's Offering

I GIVE WHAT I HAVE TO GOD. . . .

Jesus often told stories to help people understand

things like Me and heaven. Sometimes His stories

didn't make sense to everyone. And sometimes things

He said didn't always make sense to those who heard them.

One time Jesus and His disciples were watching people going into the temple. As the people went inside, they dropped their offering into a box. Many rich people put a lot of money into the offering. But a poor woman came and only put two small coins into the offering. The two coins were worth less than a penny.

Jesus told His disciples, "What I am about to tell you is true. That poor woman put more into the offering than all the others. They gave a lot of money because they are rich. But because she is poor, she gave everything she had."

Jesus was telling the disciples that what's in our hearts is more important than what we do. And because the woman wanted to give to God, she gave everything.

Snuggle Session

The poor woman gave all of her money to God
because she loved Him so much. What can you
do to show God that you love Him?

_____

_____

_____

_____

What would be the most difficult toy for you to
give away?

_____

_____

_____

My Prayer

I want to love You, God, more than anything else.
Thank You for loving me just the way I am.

God's Promise

"God loves a cheerful giver."

— 2 CORINTHIANS 9:7

Mark 10, Luke 18

Jesus Predicts His Death

THANK YOU, JESUS, THAT YOU WOULD DIE FOR ME. . . .

Jesus and His friends traveled to Jerusalem for a holiday feast. Jesus stopped and took His twelve friends aside. "When we get to Jerusalem, something is going to happen."

"What?" they asked.

"One of you will betray Me. Strangers are going to arrest Me. They will make fun of Me. They will laugh at Me, spit on Me, and kill Me. But in three days I will rise again."

Shocked, the disciples grumbled amongst themselves. They did not understand what Jesus was saying. But Jesus knew that My will would be fulfilled.

Snuggle Session

The disciples didn't like hearing Jesus talk about what was going to happen when people came to take him away. How would you feel if your best friend was moving away?

_____

_____

_____

Why is it mean to make fun of someone?

_____

_____

_____

_____

My Prayer

Dear God, help me to trust You even when life gets hard.

God's Promise

"Trust in the Lord with all your heart. Do not depend on your own understanding."

— PROVERBS 3:5

John 18–20

Jesus Dies and Rises Again

THANK YOU, JESUS, THAT YOU WILL
NEVER LEAVE US. . . .

The chief priests planned to capture Jesus, so they

asked one of His disciples, Judas, to help them. They

promised to give Judas money if he told them the place where they could find Jesus. Judas agreed, and he was given thirty silver coins.

After a special meal with His friends, Jesus and His disciples went to a place called Gethsemane to pray. While they were there, Judas led soldiers, armed with swords and clubs, to Jesus.

Peter, who loved Jesus very much, tried to save Jesus by fighting. Peter swung a sword and cut off one man's ear—but Jesus told him to put the sword away. Then Jesus healed the man and let Himself be arrested.

A man named Pilate was the ruler of the land. He knew Jesus had done nothing wrong and wanted to set Jesus free. But when the people shouted that they wanted Jesus to die, Pilate gave Him to the soldiers.

The soldiers made fun of Jesus and beat Him. They put a crown made of thorns on His head and yelled,

"Hail, King of the Jews!" They all laughed. They took Jesus to a place called Golgotha and nailed Him to a cross.

As Jesus hung there, darkness filled the land for three hours. Everything was very quiet until Jesus cried out in a loud voice and died. He died and the ones who loved Him cried.

After three days, Mary Magdalene and Mary went to visit Jesus' tomb. When they arrived, they noticed the large stone covering the entrance had been rolled away. And as they entered the tomb, they saw an angel sitting beside it—but they didn't find Jesus inside!

"Do not be afraid," the angel said. "I know you are looking for Jesus, but He is not here. He has risen, just as He said. Go tell the others." So the women went to the disciples to share the good news.

Over the next forty days, Jesus visited His friends. He

proved to them that He had risen from the dead and now lived again. One time, Jesus even ate with His friends—a snack of fish and some honey.

When the time came for Him to leave and return to heaven, He called His friends together one last time. "I am leaving, but I am sending you My Holy Spirit. My Spirit will be with you and will help you while you are here on earth. Remember, whoever believes in Me will have everlasting life. I will always be with you."

Snuggle Session

When Mary and Martha went to where Jesus was buried, an angel told them Jesus was alive. What do you think an angel looks like?

_____

_____

_____

After Jesus rose from the dead, He spent time with His friends before going to heaven. He said He was going to prepare places for those who believe in God. What do you think heaven will look like?

_____

_____

My Prayer

Dear God, thank You for Your great power that even raised Jesus from the dead.

God's Promise

"I am going there to prepare a place for you. If I go and do that, I will come back. And I will take you there to be with me. Then you will also be where I am."

— JOHN 14:2-3

Terry K. Brown is a former nurse and the creator of children's and youth product, including the popular TodaysGirls.com Web site, the *Today's Girl* book series, the communicate-christ.com Web site, and the youth devotional *Communicate*. She lives in eastern Indiana.